Instant Citrix Security How-to

A guide to bulletproofing your enterprise environment with the excellent security features in Citrix

Carmel Jacob

PUBLISHING

BIRMINGHAM - MUMBAI

Instant Citrix Security How-to

Copyright © 2013 Packt Publishing

First published: February 2013

Production Reference: 1120213

Published by Packt Publishing Ltd.
Livery Place
35 Livery Street
Birmingham B3 2PB, UK.

ISBN 978-1-84968-672-3

www.packtpub.com

Credits

Author
Carmel Jacob

Reviewer
Andrew Mallett

Acquisition Editor
Martin Bell

Commissioning Editor
Meeta Rajani

Technical Editors
Prasad Dalvi

Lubna Shaikh

Project Coordinator
Esha Thakker

Proofreader
Lawrence A. Herman

Graphics
Valentina D'silva

Production Coordinator
Melwyn D'sa

Cover Work
Melwyn D'sa

Cover Image
Sheetal Aute

About the Author

Carmel Jacob is a networking professional with five and a half years of experience and counting. She has worked on a wide range of products at different layers of networking starting with firewall, load balancers, routers, and switches. She is now into network testing and loves what she does. She has a keen interest in reading books, writing, and debugging issues at work!

I would like to express my gratitude towards my family and friends, who have been supportive and encouraging during the preparation of this book and will always be!

About the Reviewer

Andrew Mallett has worked in IT for more years than he cares to mention, well, since 1986, and is working with Citrix technologies since Metaframe 1.8 in 1999. He not only has Citrix skills and certification, but also teaches Linux, Citrix, Novell, and Microsoft official courses and supports many of these products. He is well versed and certified in Linux. His interest and skills in security and remote access made this book an ideal book for him to review. He has also authored the book *Citrix Access Gateway VPX 5.04 Essentials*, *Packt Publishing*, which you may want to look at yourself.

Andrew currently works for QA Ltd. (`http://www.qa.com`), the largest Citrix authorized learning center in the U.K., as a Certified Citrix Instructor and Principal Technologist. You may well find Andrew teaching across the U.K. at one of their many training centers.

www.PacktPub.com

Support files, eBooks, discount offers and more

You might want to visit www.PacktPub.com for support files and downloads related to your book.

Did you know that Packt offers eBook versions of every book published, with PDF and ePub files available? You can upgrade to the eBook version at www.PacktPub.com and as a print book customer, you are entitled to a discount on the eBook copy. Get in touch with us at service@ packtpub.com for more details.

At www.PacktPub.com, you can also read a collection of free technical articles, sign up for a range of free newsletters and receive exclusive discounts and offers on Packt books and eBooks.

http://PacktLib.PacktPub.com

Do you need instant solutions to your IT questions? PacktLib is Packt's online digital book library. Here, you can access, read and search across Packt's entire library of books.

Why Subscribe?

- ▸ Fully searchable across every book published by Packt
- ▸ Copy and paste, print and bookmark content
- ▸ On demand and accessible via wcb browser

Free Access for Packt account holders

If you have an account with Packt at www.PacktPub.com, you can use this to access PacktLib today and view nine entirely free books. Simply use your login credentials for immediate access.

Instant Updates on New Packt Books

Get notified! Find out when new books are published by following @PacktEnterprise on Twitter, or the *Packt Enterprise* Facebook page.

Table of Contents

Preface

"My books are like water; those of the great geniuses are wine. (Fortunately) everybody drinks water."

—Mark Twain

The aim of this book is to comb through the many features of Citrix Application Delivery Controller, which is NetScaler, and give you insight into how to handle and tune them according to your requirements.

I have tried to whip up as many recipes as possible so that they would be easier for readers to choose from. In addition, there are certain important terms explained, which we usually come across while deploying Citrix NetScalers and Access Gateways, but don't think much about. By the end of this book, we hope to give readers a good practical knowledge of the working of an end-to-end Citrix solution. Though it is recommended you read it from start to finish, it is made flexible so that you can move between recipes and skip to recipes that intrigue you.

This book will also try to simplify any complexities involved and make the read an interesting one.

I would like to sign off with a quote from Bruce Lee (I'm a big fan!).

"Use only that which works, and take it from any place you can find it."

—Bruce Lee

What this book covers

Day one – deployment in a DMZ network (Must know) discusses the basic set up of NetScaler in DMZ and the server farm in internal zone, while keeping in mind what changes should be done to ensure connectivity between NetScaler and the backend servers.

Triple A (Must know) shows how to configure the AAA vserver and use it with CS/LB vserver. This recipe also shows the readers how to configure SSO functionality and gives the readers a detailed packet flow as well as a capture that shows a successful authentication using LDAP, which can be used to troubleshoot in readers' environments.

Controlling surge/burst (Must know) shows how to enable settings that turn on surge protection, along with the base threshold and throttling options. This recipe also explains how the protection works along with NetScaler's inherent connection multiplexing.

Content switching (Must know) discusses a simple but most commonly used procedure to redirect the HTTP traffic to secure HTTPS by using the responder policy bound to the CS level along with the configuration commands.

Zombie cleanup (Must know) discusses how to clean up idle connections that would take up space and memory at intervals that can be customized. This recipe also shows the levels at which the timeout can be set.

Disaster recovery (Should know) introduces a series of steps for setting up disaster recovery and later shows the ways to troubleshoot it as well. This recipe includes a discussion of dynamic proximity, which shows how the RTT calculation is done. This recipe also discusses the steps that are used to calculate as well as configure dynamic proximity.

DOS and attack prevention (Should know) covers default settings that provide protection along with the options that can be turned on to provide extra security. This recipe throws light on how to set up priority queuing for different types of traffic among other things. Rate limiting configuration is also included in the recipe.

Learning Application Firewall (Must know) guides the readers through the steps and shows snapshots of the defense mechanism with the help of logs and packet captures. It also speaks about role-based access control where you can restrict the management access of a user to the desired level. This recipe also includes tips to troubleshoot the App Firewall issue.

The Access Gateway integration for Citrix XenApp and XenDesktop (Become an expert) focuses on basic and smart access modes, explaining each of them briefly with the options each mode can provide to the users. There are a few knobs in Access Gateway, which are highlighted in this recipe. As with all the recipes, this one too has a troubleshooting section.

Network management (Must know) explains how a user can use the built-in reporting software and dashboard that Citrix NetScaler device provides. It also briefly speaks about the command center software.

What you need for this book

This book is mostly written with the help of Citrix NetScaler VPX with basic licenses. But as you know there are a few features (for example, GSLB and so on) that would need a full-fledged licensed appliance. So before you start, to make the best use of the appliance, make sure you have all the necessary licenses.

For more details on licenses, you can get in touch with customer care at `http://citrix.com/support`.

If the intention is to learn and perform non-production tests, you can proceed with the NetScaler VPX software that is freely available on the Citrix homepage (`http://www.citrix.com`).

Who this book is for

The target audience is mainly the networking professionals and more importantly ones who are planning to deploy a single device that takes care of load balancing/VPN/App Firewall. This also applies to users who already have an existing environment and are unsure of how to proceed.

This book serves as a manual as well as a reference with useful tips and tricks; it is meant to be as practical as possible, keeping in mind real-life scenarios.

Conventions

In this book, you will find a number of styles of text that distinguish between different kinds of information. Here are some examples of these styles, and an explanation of their meaning.

Code words in text are shown as follows: "At this time, the `<show lb server>` output will show round robin as the current method."

A block of code is set as follows:

```
GET /Test.xml?<script>alert(hi)</script> HTTP/1.1
Accept: application/x-ms-application, image/jpeg, application/
xaml+xml, image/gif, image/pjpeg, application/x-ms-xbap, application/
x-shockwave-flash, application/vnd.ms-excel, application/vnd.ms-
powerpoint, application/msword, */*
Accept-Language: en-US
User-Agent: Mozilla/4.0 (compatible; MSIE 8.0; Windows NT 6.1; WOW64;
Trident/4.0; SLCC2; .NET CLR 2.0.50727; .NET CLR 3.5.30729; .NET CLR
3.0.30729; Media Center PC 6.0; InfoPath.3)
Accept-Encoding: gzip, deflate
Host: www.packttest.com
Connection: Keep-Alive
Cookie: citrix_ns_id=SQIoGifoC0oF+GaOVYl3cCJDKTQA000
```

```
HTTP/1.1 200 OK
Pragma: "no-cache"
Content-Length: 99
Connection: close
<html>
<head>
     <title>THIS PAGE IS BLOCKED BY CITRIX APPLICAITON FIREWALL
   </title>
  </head>
</html>
```

Any command-line input or output is written as follows:

```
add ns simpleacl  packtacl DENY -srcIP  10.122.23.40  -destPort
1494 -protocol TCP
```

New terms and **important words** are shown in bold. Words that you see on the screen, in menus or dialog boxes for example, appear in the text like this: "Go to **Load Balancing | Virtual Servers**."

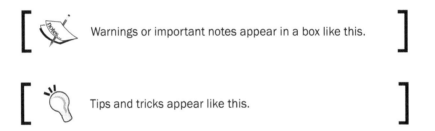

Warnings or important notes appear in a box like this.

Tips and tricks appear like this.

Reader feedback

Feedback from our readers is always welcome. Let us know what you think about this book—what you liked or may have disliked. Reader feedback is important for us to develop titles that you really get the most out of.

To send us general feedback, simply send an e-mail to feedback@packtpub.com, and mention the book title via the subject of your message.

If there is a book that you need and would like to see us publish, please send us a note in the **SUGGEST A TITLE** form on www.packtpub.com or e-mail suggest@packtpub.com.

If there is a topic that you have expertise in and you are interested in either writing or contributing to a book, see our author guide on www.packtpub.com/authors.

Customer support

Now that you are the proud owner of a Packt book, we have a number of things to help you to get the most from your purchase.

Errata

Although we have taken every care to ensure the accuracy of our content, mistakes do happen. If you find a mistake in one of our books—maybe a mistake in the text or the code—we would be grateful if you would report this to us. By doing so, you can save other readers from frustration and help us improve subsequent versions of this book. If you find any errata, please report them by visiting http://www.packtpub.com/support, selecting your book, clicking on the **errata submission form** link, and entering the details of your errata. Once your errata are verified, your submission will be accepted and the errata will be uploaded on our website, or added to any list of existing errata, under the Errata section of that title. Any existing errata can be viewed by selecting your title from http://www.packtpub.com/support.

Piracy

Piracy of copyright material on the Internet is an ongoing problem across all media. At Packt Publishing, we take the protection of our copyright and licenses very seriously. If you come across any illegal copies of our works, in any form, on the Internet, please provide us with the location address or website name immediately so that we can pursue a remedy.

Please contact us at copyright@packtpub.com with a link to the suspected pirated material.

We appreciate your help in protecting our authors, and our ability to bring you valuable content.

Questions

You can contact us at questions@packtpub.com if you are having a problem with any aspect of the book, and we will do our best to address it.

Instant Citrix Security How-to

Beef up your network security with Citrix!

With millions of devices being plugged in to the Internet, more and more computing tasks are now handled online, from providing secure payment gateways to downloading entertainment to personalized search engines. This book aims at going past antivirus patches and encrypted communication that earlier summed up a secure environment. It walks you through setting up an end-to-end Citrix solution, highlighting the security features that each has to offer.

Day one – deployment in a DMZ network (Must know)

Implementing a **De-Militarized Zone** (**DMZ**) within any network is a good measure to protect servers that are on an internal or trusted network. This recipe will show a step-by-step implementation of NetScaler in a single-hop DMZ environment and multi-hop DMZ setup.

Getting ready

The Citrix NetScaler and Access Gateway are one and the same device but with different licenses. The Access Gateway functionality can be enabled with the Access Gateway universal license. The universal license, by default, enables five users to connect concurrently. Additional concurrent user licenses can be obtained for the number required (for example, a 100-user license).

Before the task begins, please make sure you have configured NetScaler with the Netscaler IP address, that is for management purposes (it will prompt in the initial configuration), and without which you will not be able to access the device. Also, the latest NetScaler devices come with two management interfaces; take care to not plug them into the same virtual local area network (VLAN), which would cause loops and broadcast storms.

How to do it...

Inbound Internet traffic to your network should be avoided at all costs; hence it is always recommended to set up NetScaler in a DMZ zone that is isolated from the trusted network (your internal network) and the Internet. It acts as a buffer zone between two enemies and does not allow direct contact between them.

This can be achieved by physically locating the web servers that will be accessed by the public network in a different subnet and by blocking any traffic from going beyond the DMZ to the trust zone, or by configuring the internal and DMZ subnets in two different VLANs, or having NetScaler's legs in two boats—one in DMZ and the other in the trust network. We shall discuss each of these options in the following recipes:

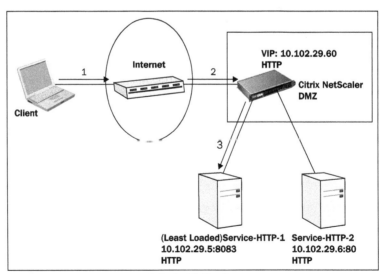

LB-Basic_LB_Topology

We will now be configuring the DMZ and internal zone in different VLANs:

1. Configure the virtual server IPs that are accessible over the Internet. The client reaches out to this IP address and establishes a TCP connection in order to access the backend servers.

2. Configure the VIP and its corresponding services and the server object applicable.

3. Go to **Load Balancing | Virtual Servers**:

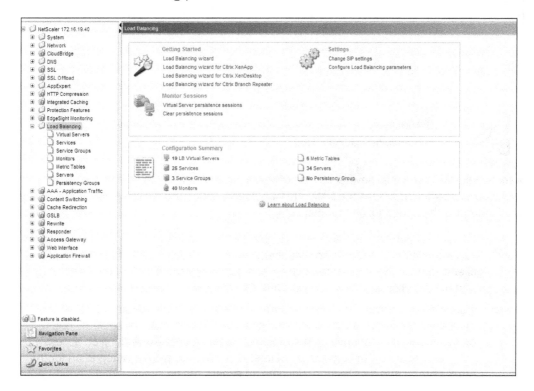

By default, NetScaler assigns monitors to each of the services configured; load balancing, by default, is the least connection.

Please note to configure **Subnet-IPs** (**SNIPs**) while creating multiple VLANs and bind them to the respective VLANs.

We will now configure SNIP/MIP.

Go to **System** | **Networking** | **IP** (here you can see all the types of configured and configurable IPs):

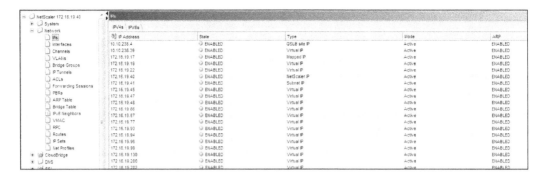

 SNIP/MIP should be configured in the same subnet as the backend servers that are being load balanced.

A multi-hop DMZ setup has several layers of firewall protection that provide extra security to the internal network. It divides the DMZ into two stages, hence two access gateways need to be deployed in this scenario, one for each stage:

1. The access gateway needs to be configured with a default gateway or static routes to reach the internal network, so that users can access resources in the network. When clients connect, they can access the resources using the Citrix XenApp online plugin and not the access gateway plugin. Only ICA traffic is supported in this setup.

2. A simple way to accomplish this is to run the access gateway wizard, which will help in creating the virtual server and binding the certificates. External servers need to be configured for authentication and authorization. A detailed working on access gateway integration will be discussed later in the access gateway integration for the *Citrix XenApp and XenDesktop (Become an expert)* recipe.

How it works...

The first recipe is pretty straightforward and has NetScaler in the DMZ and the server farm in the internal network. The VIP will be configured with a public IP and we can further restrict its access to the Internet by applying ACLs and also making use of external authentication.

In the second option, the access gateway in the first DMZ receives the client connections and redirects these connections to the web interface in the second DMZ. The access gateway in the second DMZ is a proxy that allows ICA traffic to traverse the second DMZ, to reach the backend server farm.

There's more...

This section dwells on a few miniscule must-know facts on the Citrix NetScaler and its deployment.

NetScaler load balancing (slow start)

Whenever the load balancing method is selected as metric-based (for example, least connection), NetScaler initially starts with **Round Robin** for what is known as the slow start period. For each new server added, it will initially be round robin for the slow start period. At this time, the `<show lb server>` output will show round robin as the current method.

Licenses

In the **NetScaler Configuration Utility GUI** under **System | Licenses**, there will be a tick mark for all the licenses that are activated in the box. Features that are not enabled but have licenses would be shown as **Capture_notenabled:**

Capture_notenabled.

The licenses can be downloaded from My Citrix (`http://citrix.com/downloads`).

Triple A (Must know)

The first thought that comes to mind when somebody says **AAA**? Batteries? Credit Ratings? No, it is the user **authentication**, **authorization**, and **auditing** feature, and it is all about having Netscaler/access gateway to manage access controls rather than an admin managing the access controls separately for each app. This recipe shows how NetScaler controls the access for the XenApp farms on your private network.

Getting ready

To configure AAA on NetScaler, you need to start by creating an SSL certificate-key pair and bind it to the AAA **vserver** (the certificate request and the key can be generated on NetScaler and submitted to the **Certificate Authority,** also knows as **CA,** to receive the cert-key pair). The AAA vserver should then be associated with any traffic-management vserver (load balancing [LB] or content switching [CS]). DNS needs to be configured to assign hostnames to both the AAA vserver and the traffic management vserver; please note that both the hostnames should be in the same domain, while creating the cert-key pair uses the appropriate domain in the subject name. (Self-signed certificates will not work for AAA, as they are used for testing purpose only.) The procedure of configuring a cert-key request and binding it to a vserver and the DNS configuration will be shown in detail in the following sections of this chapter.

The AAA functionality can be used for simple traffic management as well as for virtual private network (VPN) functionality!

How to do it...

Triple A comes across as an important feature of the Citrix Netscaler, as it can be used from a simple load balancing environment to VPN, coupled with a wide range of external authentication types. In this section, we shall see how to set up a AAA vserver from scratch that can be bound to a LB or Content Switching vserver:

1. Create a cert-key pair by configuring the certificate signing request on NetScaler. Go to **SSL**, click on **Certificate Signing Request (CSR)**, and follow the instructions to generate a CSR. Similarly, you can create the RSA key. After generating the CSR and key, both need to be submitted to the CA, which in turn will produce the cert-key pair. The cert-key pair then needs to be loaded on the NetScaler box through SCP/FTP and so on.

2. Configure the AAA vserver and bind the cert-key pair to it. In the AAA vserver, the **Authentication** tab is where the external authentication profile and policy needs to be configured. We can use any flavor of LDAP or RADIUS. Further more, you can add a session policy to increase/decrease the timeouts and the **Single sign-on (SSO)** functionality to the web applications.

> With SSO, a user has to log in just once and he would have access to multiple different applications and systems. The user credentials will be internally stored and these credentials will be granted to the applications that request them.

To add the SSO functionality, run the following commands:

```
>add tm sessionAction <sso_act > -SSO ON -ssoCredential PRIMARY
-ssoDomain aaa.test.com
>add tm sessionPolicy <sson-act_pol> ns_true sson
>bind authentication vserver AAA-vip -policy sson-pol -priority 1
Done
```

3. The AAA vserver is then bound to the **LB or CS** server. The LB/CS vserver should be on HTTP and on the **Advanced** tab of the traffic management server. The authentication vserver needs to be bound and the domain name of the AAA vserver should be specified. The following screenshot shows the CLI output of the LB vserver after the configuration and binding of the the AAA vservers:

```
> show lb vserver ▮▮▮▮▮▮▮▮▮▮▮▮▮
        172.16.▮▮.▮▮_80 (172.16.19.22:80) – HTTP           Type: ADDRESS
        State: UP
        Last state change was at Sat Sep 22 08:57:25 2012
        Time since last state change: 0 days, 00:00:14.920
        Effective State: UP
        Client Idle Timeout: 180 sec
        Down state flush: DISABLED
        Disable Primary Vserver On Down : DISABLED
        Appflow logging: DISABLED
        Port Rewrite : DISABLED
        No. of Bound Services :  1 (Total)          1 (Active)
        Configured Method: LEASTCONNECTION
        Current Method: Round Robin, Reason: A new service is bound
        Mode: IP
        Persistence: NONE
        Vserver IP and Port insertion: OFF
        Authentication: ON        Host: abecag.▮▮▮▮.lab
        401 Based Authentication: OFF    Authn Vserver: aaavserver.▮▮▮▮.lab
        Push: DISABLED  Push VServer:
        Push Multi Clients: NO
        Push Label Rule: none
        L2Conn: OFF
        Skip Persistency: None
        IcmpResponse: PASSIVE
1) ▮▮▮▮▮▮▮▮▮▮▮Service (127.0.0.1: 8080) – HTTP State: UP    Weight: 1
```

How it works...

A step-by-step working of the client to server authentication through Netscaler will be shown using HTTP headers (an HTTP header trace taken on the IE browser was used for the setup here):

1. The client sends an HTTP request to the LB vserver, the LB vserver sends a 302 redirect to the AAA vserver.

    In this case, we can see that www.a.abc.com and www.abc.com belong to the same domain name.

    The following code is the output of an HTTP header trace taken during the authentication phase (a simple HTTP header trace or a Mozilla header tool that can be downloaded for capturing the HTTP headers):

```
GET / HTTP/1.1

Host: a.abc.com

User-Agent: Mozilla/5.0 (Windows NT 6.1; rv:14.0) Gecko/20100101
Firefox/14.0.1

Accept: text/html,application/xhtml+xml,application/
xml;q=0.9,*/*;q=0.8

Accept-Language: en-gb,en;q=0.5

Accept-Encoding: gzip, deflate

Connection: keep-alive
```

```
HTTP/1.1 200 OK

Content-Length:681

Cache-control: no-cache, no-store

Pragma: no-cache

Content-Type: text/html
```

2. The AAA vserver then sends a page to the client for getting the authentication credentials:

   HTTP Header trace:

```
POST /cgi/tm HTTP/1.1

Accept: image/jpeg,*/*

Accept-Language: en-US

User-Agent: Mozilla/4.0 (compatible; MSIE 8.0; Windows NT 6.1;

Content-Type: application/x-www-form-urlencoded

Accept-Encoding: gzip, deflate

Host: abc.com

Content-Length: 55

Connection: Keep-Alive

Cache-Control: no-cache

Referer:

HTTP/1.1 302 Object Moved

Location: /vpn/tmindex.html

Set-Cookie: NSC_TASS=03110d1ceac81fd1f5317e3415d75c58;Secure;HttpO
nly;Path=/

Set-Cookie: NSC_TEMP=xyz;Path=/;expires=Wednesday, 09-Nov-1999
23:12:40

Set-Cookie: NSC_TEMP=xyz;Path=/;Domain=apac.lab;expires=Wednesday,
09-Nov

Connection: close

Content-Length: 536

Cache-control: no-cache, no-store

Pragma: no-cache

Content-Type: text/html


GET /vpn/tmindex.html HTTP/1.1

Accept: image/jpeg, application/x-ms-application, image/
gif, application/xaml+xml, image/pjpeg, application/x-ms-xbap,
application/x-shockwave-flash, application/vnd.ms-powerpoint,
```

```
application/vnd.ms-excel, application/msword, */*

Accept-Language: en-AU

User-Agent: Mozilla/4.0 (compatible; MSIE 8.0; Windows NT 6.1;

Cookie: NSC_TMAA=802662f5eb2a319f29b9af61086313f3; NSC_TMAS=b8e51a
409ec3c39541378edb91e80d50; NSC_TASS=03110d1ceac81fd1f5317e3415d7
5c58

Accept-Encoding: gzip, deflate

Host: abc.com

Connection: Keep-Alive

Cache-Control: no-cache

Referer:


HTTP/1.1 200 OK

Date: Sat, 22 Sep 2012 08:39:45 GMT

Server: Apache

Last-Modified: Tue, 11 Sep 2012 22:48:07 GMT

ETag: "40f8-16ae-4c974de21f7c0"

Accept-Ranges: bytes

Content-Length: 5806

Keep-Alive: timeout=15, max=100

Connection: Keep-Alive

Content-Type: text/html

Cache-Control: no-cache
```

After the authentication is successful, the client gets redirected back to the LB vserver. This time, the AAA sends a cookie to the client so that the subsequent requests from the client would contain the same cookie. NetScaler looks at the cookies and directs the request to the appropriate backend service (according to the LB method configured). At any point in time, the following screenshot shows the CLI command, which when entered will show the number of active users connected:

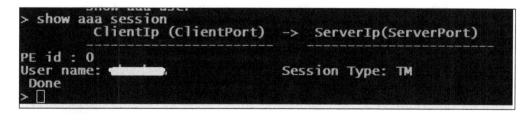

The following diagram is a pictorial representation of the authentication request between the LB and AAA vserver:

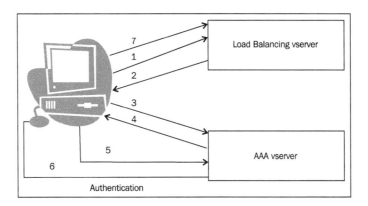

There's more...

This section will throw some light on debugging the external authentication issue.

 The **ns-server certificate** present on NetScaler is used only for secure management access of NetScaler. The management access can be restricted to HTTPS (secure) only, or both HTTP and HTTPS. Similarly, you can add either MIP or SNIP for a GUI secure access.

Tips and troubleshooting

There are a few common issues that could be listed for for AAA:

▸ The certificate has to be trusted; if you are connecting with a security exception, AAA will not work. Another important note would be to check for certificate expiry.

▸ The NSC_TMAA cookie should be preserved by the browser for successive transactions by the client in either the same or different browsers. This can be verified by taking an ethereal or wireshark capture on the client machine.

▸ When there are multiple applications that need to be accessed in the same session and each of them open a new connection, the client might face an issue of authenticating multiple times. The same holds true if the browser is not able to preserve the cookie. In such conditions, there is an option on NetScaler to enable persistent cookies. This setting is available globally or can be restricted to only certain traffic policies that are be bound to the AAA vserver.

The following is a CLI command to enable persistent cookie setting on NetScaler for AAA traffic:

```
>set tm sessionParameter -SSO ON -httpOnlyCookie NO -persistentCookie
ENABLED -persistentCookieValidity 30 [GLOBAL SETTING]
```

The following is a CLI command to enable a debug for AAA(CLI):

```
>shell
```

```
#cd /tmp
```

```
#cat aaad.debug [This command would enable aaad debug,to stop its press
Ctrl+Z]
```

The following screenshot shows the debug logs for a successful authentication:

Controlling surge/burst (Must know)

Handling massive surges in traffic is extremely important for organizations that do their business in websites. Even for others, sudden bursts in traffic do not come fully announced and need to be taken care of. This section deals with how the Citrix NetScaler controls and regulates traffic, thereby preventing outages.

Getting ready

The surge protection feature of NetScaler is enabled either globally or at service level. This feature controls the number of simultaneous connections made by NetScaler to the backend server farm. Surge protection is enabled by default and hence for scenarios where surge protection is not necessary it needs to be disabled. Surge protection should not be enabled when the **Use Source IP** (**USIP**) mode is enabled because with the USIP mode the number of backend connections will increase, as the original client IP will be shown as the source IP, and hence connection re-use is ruled out. Therefore, when more and more connections form, surge protection will get aggressive and not work as expected.

How to do it...

Setting up surge protection on NetScaler is a very simple procedure. As discussed before, it is enabled by default on the NetScaler GUI. It can be found under **System | Settings | Global System Settings**:

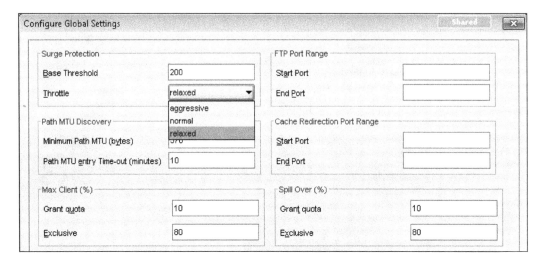

By default, two values are set:

▶ **Base Threshold** is the maximum number of concurrent connections that NetScaler will forward to the backend servers before triggering the surge protection. For each Throttle value, a predefined numbered set that can be changed.

▶ **Throttle** can be normal, aggressive, or relaxed, each having a predefined number of connections that can be changed.

At service level, we have the surge protection checkbox under **Advanced | Settings | Surge Protection**:

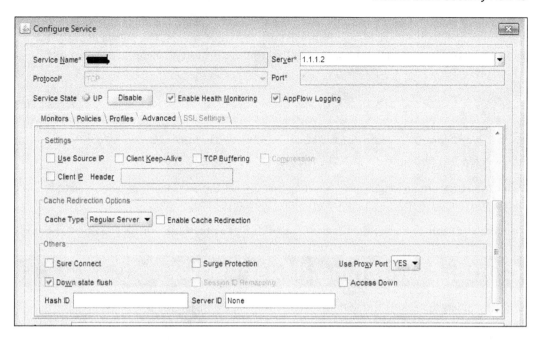

How it works...

It is important to keep the server functioning at a normal capacity, as overloading it may result in undesirable results, such as application crashes and unavailability of resources for clients. NetScaler's basic functionality is connection multiplexing between the client and server (per request based). Hence, whenever a new connection is made and surge protection is enabled, it would check for any free existing connection to the servers; if not, then according to the max client and max request value set at the service level, the connection will be served or put in the surge queue.

The length of the surge queue will decrease if any existing connection in the backend becomes free.

There's more...

This section deals with certain tidbits that will come in handy with respect to surge protection.

If the rate at which requests hit NetScaler increase exponentially, the surge queue will become longer, hence it will be necessary to flush the surge queue. The following are a few simple network management protocol OIDs that retrieve the length of surge queue at the vserver level:

- `vsvrSurgeCount,1.3.6.1.4.1.5951.4.1.3.1.1.10`
- `surgeCount,1.3.6.1.4.1.5951.1.4.1.1.1.7`
- `tcpSurgeQueueLen,1.3.6.1.4.1.5951.4.1.1.46.15`
- `svcSurgeCount,1.3.6.1.4.1.5951.4.1.2.1.1.10`

When the surge queue length becomes long and affects the availability of resources to the users, you can flush the surge queue with the following CLI command:

`root@ns> flush ns surgeQ [-name <name>] [-serverName <serverName> <port>]`

Content switching (Must know)

CS is the ability to redirect traffic based on content file extensions and, going a step further, in redirecting based on geographical locations. Multiple hostnames can be mapped to the same CS VIP using the server name indication feature from NetScaler 9.2 onwards. Starting with the NetScaler version 10 software, the version of MySQL software can be set for content switching virtual servers (this is to avoid compatibility problems between the client and server). This section deals with the implementation of content switching.

Getting ready

We will start with the packet flow of NetScaler and where content switching comes into play. The following diagram is self-explanatory (it is not the entire packet flow to the receiver's endpoint; the focus here is only to CS and LB):

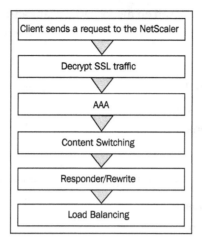

The content switching vserver can be used for HTTP/HTTPS/TCP and UDP protocols, and it can direct it only to another vserver, not to the backend service directly.

The content switching vserver doesn't need an LB vserver to be bound to it for its status to be UP. Even with nothing bound to the CS vserver, the status would show UP (this comes in handy when you want to blackhole unwanted traffic).Hence, it is always recommended to check whether the load balancing vservers that are bound to the content switching vserver are up and running.

If you want to avoid the preceding condition, the following CLI command will help you achieve it (by default, the value is disabled):

```
root@ NetScaler> add cs vserver <name> <serviceType> (<IPAddress>)
[-stateupdate ( ENABLED | DISABLED )]
```

Content switching can be done based on the following client attributes:

- ▶ Mobile user/PC
- ▶ Images/videos
- ▶ Dynamic/static content
- ▶ Client with/without cookies
- ▶ Geographical locations.
- ▶ Per VLAN

Similarly, server-side differentiations can also be made based on the following attributes:

- ▶ Server speed and capacity
- ▶ Source/destination port
- ▶ Source/destination IP
- ▶ SSL/HTTP

Citrix also has an additional feature (starting from NetScaler version 9.3) that dynamically selects the load balancing feature based on any criteria or condition provided in the CS action/policy:

```
>add cs action <name> -targetLBVserver <string-expression>
>add cs policy <policyName> -rule <RULEValue> -action <actionName>
```

The policy is then bound to the CS vserver

> CS vservers can be configured to process URLs in a case-sensitive manner. By default, this option is ON:
>
> ```
> >set cs vserver CSVserver -caseSensitive ON
> ```

The load balancing vserver bound to the CS vserver need not have any IP address configured unless it is used in a different access as well.

How to do it...

We shall focus on a few case studies that we commonly come across, and that can be solved with the help of content switching:

Case 1: Customer ABC accesses an online shopping portal and gets redirected to a secure connection at the payment gateway. For this scenario, an HTTP LB vserver is used and is bound to the CS vserver, which is on HTTPS:

```
root@ns>add cs vserver testVserver HTTPS 10.10.1.1 443
Done
root@ns>add cs policy CS_Policy -rule "http.req.method.eq(GET)" -
action act1
Done
root@ns>add responder action CS_http_https redirect"https://"+
HTTP.REQ.HOSTNAME.HTTP_HEADER_SAFE +
HTTP.REQ.URL.PATH_AND_QUERY.HTTP_URL_SAFE
Done
root@ns>add responder policy pol1
HTTP.REQ.HOSTNAME.CONTAINS("www.abc.com")
&& HTTP.REQ.URL.CONTAINS("/payement/") CS_http_https
Done
root@ns>bind cs vserver csw_vserv lb_vserver1 -policyName
csw_pol_portal1 -priority 100
Done
```

The configuration in the preceding screenshot shows that a CS policy as well as a responder policy is bound to the CS vserver named `testVserver`.

The CS policy works on directing the traffic to the target LB vserver (if there are no CS policies bound at all, it goes to the default LB vserver; this default LB vserver should be configured on the CS Vserver). The responder policy, if bound to the CS vserver works on HTTP requests before matching any CS policy.

The configuration is verified by using show `cs vserver <vserver name>`. A packet capture taken on NetScaler will clearly show the redirect from HTTP to HTTPS as `<HTTP 302>`.

If there is any traffic that doesn't match any specific CS policies that are bound, then it uses the default policy. If there is no default policy, the user will get an error – `HTTP 1.1 Service Unavailable error message`.

Case 2: The customer Star Networks has a single web application that contains two domains, namely `www.starnetworks.com` and `www.starnetworks.com.edu` and has a content switching setup, which works fine when accessing `www.starnetworks.com`, but throws an error when accessing `www.starnetworks.com.edu`.

This happens because the peceding domains are not the same; they are different and the certificate that is bound to the CS vserver would be of type `www.starnetworks.com` only. To resolve this issue, we can bind multiple certificates to the CS vserver with the **Server Name Indication** (**SNI**) option enabled. The SNI option can be enabled in the **SSL Parameters** tab (this would pop up only if the SSL protocol is chosen while creating the vserver).

The CLI command to enable SNI is as follows:

```
>bind sslvserver star_cs_vserver -certkeyname    -SNICert
> bind sslvserver star_cs_vserver -certkeyname    -SNICert
```

For each domain added, NetScaler will establish a secure channel between itself and the client. With this solution, you can avoid configuring multiple CS vservers.

Case 3: A Customer has a large pool of IP subnets that needs categorizing, and it would be a next to impossible task to configure that number of content switching policies; how does he go about deploying this scenario?

The solution is as follows:

1. A database file should be created that includes the IP address range and the domain:

   ```
   >shell
   #cd /var/ NetScaler/locdb
   # vi test.db
   ```

   (Here, the `gslb` entries are added, which will be discussed in detail in the *Disaster recovery (Should know)* recipe.)

2. Run the following command to apply the changes made to the database file:

   ```
   > add locationfile aol.db
   ```

3. Bind the CS policy with an expression stating, for example, as follows:

   ```
   "CLIENT.IP.SRC.MATCHES_LOCATION (\"star.*.*.*.*.*\")""
   ```

How it works...

The working of NetScaler in all three preceding scenarios is that it analyzes the incoming traffic directed to the CS VIP and parses through the bound CS policies, if any. If a match is found, it goes to the target LB vserver. If there are any other policies that are bound (for example, a responder policy or a rewrite policy), then the responder policy gets executed even before the CS policy is executed (since responder policies are usually applied to the HTTP requests).However, rewrite policies can be bound either at the CS or LB level, depending on whether the request or response needs to be modified.

To recap what we have seen in the case studies mentioned before, the first case helps us to do a simple redirect from HTTP to HTTPS using a responder policy bound at the CS level. The second case shows us how multiple certificates with the SNI option are used to solve domain differences that would otherwise cause issues. The final case study shows us the basic but handy setting to map IP address ranges to target load balancing vservers. An important thing to note – there are scenarios where the vserver and the services that are bound to them may be different ports altogether (for example, HTTP LB VIP would be listening on port 80, but the services would be on port 8080). In such cases, the `redirectPortRewrite` feature should be enabled.

There's more...

This section concentrates on tidbits and troubleshooting techniques:

Tips and troubleshooting

1. We can start with checking the output of `show cs` and `show lb vservers`, to see if the services bound to them are up and running:

   ```
   root@ns > show cs vserver cs_star_vserver


                       1) cs_star_vserver (IP_ADDRESS_HERE:80) - HTTP
   Type: CONTENT
                       State: UP
                       Client Idle Timeout: 180 sec
                   Down state flush: ENABLED
               Port Rewrite : DISABLED
                       Default: lb_vserver          Content
   Precedence:                 RULE
                       Vserver IP and Port insertion: OFF
                       Case Sensitivity: OFF
   ```

2. If there are responder and rewrite policies, then we can check whether the number of hits on that policy are incrementing or not.

3. Packet captures (using Wireshark) on the server and NetScaler. In some cases, the client would show us the packet flow in depth.

4. The **Down state flush** feature of the NetScaler is useful for admins planning their downtimes in advance. This feature is enabled, by default, on the vserver and service level. When the feature is enabled, the connections that are already open and established will be terminated and the users will have to retry their connections again. The requests that are already being processed alone would be honored. When the feature is disabled, the open and established connections are honored, and no new connections will be accepted at this time. If enabled at the vserver level, and if the state of the vserver is DOWN, then the vserver will flush the client and server connections that are linked. Otherwise, it would terminate only the client facing connections. At the server level, if the service is marked as DOWN, then only the server facing connections would be flushed.

5. There is another option on the **Advanced** tab of the CS/LB vserver to direct the excess traffic to a backup vserver. In cases where the backup server also overflows, there is an option to use the redirect URL, which is also found in the **Advanced** tab of the CS/LB vserver.

Zombie cleanup (Must know)

To avoid idle connections over an extended period of time, NetScaler used the zombie cleanup feature. Instead of immediately terminating the connections, this feature puts the idle connections into a collection pool. When consequent client requests are made, these requests are served with the idle connections that were in the re-use pool; therefore, TCP handshakes and terminations need not be done frequently with the backend servers, which in turn leads to minimizing CPU and resources on the NetScaler. The connection multiplexing happens only on the HTTP VIP and not just on any TCP VIP. Even though connection multiplexing is done at the TCP level, it is not supported for all types of traffic running over TCP. HTTP and SSL are the only two types that support connection multiplexing.

Connection multiplexing works as shown in the following screenshot:

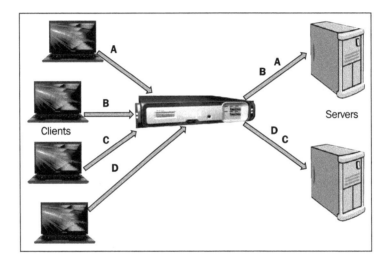

NetScaler has a pool of active connections to the server called the re-use pool; the number of connections in the re-use pool can be seen by using the following `nsconmsg` command:

```
shell# nsconmsg -s ConLb=2 -d oldconmsg
```

The output will have values such as OE (xx), SQ (x), and RP (x), where **OE** is **Open Established** connections, **SQ** is **Surge Queue**, and **RP** is **Re-use Pool**.

A common query that crops up is whether re-use is supported with USIP enabled. Yes, it is supported (only for HTTP) as NetScaler still acts as a proxy, and using its own MAC address it only inserts the client's IP address. Hence, in conditions where the source IP is from a large proxy, we would still be able to re-use connections. However, care should be taken to see that the CPU does not spike.

Getting ready

The most common problems faced without zombie cleanup is a drop in traffic, and slow responses and requests (page timeouts). This also could lead to high CPU usage, since the idle and inactive connections that are not cleaned up would only lead to unwanted usage of the resources. DOS attacks can be saved for a different chapter altogether, but certain types of attacks can be prevented using the zombie cleanup feature of NetScaler.

How to do it...

The time interval to be set in the zombie process is as follows:

```
root@ns>set ns timeout -zombie 140     (By default zombie timeout is 120)
```

In the GUI interface, it is under **System | Change timeout values**. At each level of configuration (that is, at the vserver, service, and server level) a client timeout can be configured to notify the zombie process to kick in once the timeout has expired.

For example, at the vserver level this command sets the time up to which NetScaler leaves the connection in the re-use pool:

```
root@ns>set vserver PacktLB_vserver -cltTimeout 120
```

How it works...

Once the connections are in the re-use pool, the zombie timer kicks in and cleans up the connections once the timer has expired. There is a knob to disable the zombie cleanup:

```
set service "PACKT_service" -maxreq 1
```

This setting disables connection multiplexing as well. There would be a one-to-one mapping between the client and server.

Therefore, this setting in NetScaler is enabled by default for an interval of 120 seconds; it can be customized to suit our requirement, though in most cases it is recommended to leave it at default.

Disaster recovery (Should know)

Imagine load balancing a pair of NetScaler devices across geographical locations, so that traffic is always passing through, irrespective of whether it uses the main site or an alternate site (during major outages or if there is an excess load of traffic) based on the selected LB algorithms; that is GSLB for you. This section briefs about setting up the GSLB disaster recovery.

Getting ready

NetScaler can be set up in many different ways for GSLB, some of which are listed as follows:

1. NetScaler as the **Authoritative DNS** (**ADNS**) server (by configuring a service on DNS port number 53)

2. NetScaler as Authoritative subdomain name server (by assigning a part of the domain alone to NS)

3. NS as the DNS proxy (by configuring the LB vserver and binding DNS servers to it)

Starting from NetScaler version 10, even with static proximity configured, there is an option to override the static mapping of location database with a specific DNS policy, and action to direct the traffic coming from a specific **Local DNS** (**LDNS**) server, or network to specific gslb services. Follow the next screenshot to statically configure the IP address and location database on GUI.

On the **Configuration Utility** panel, go to **GSLB | Location** to create static location entries:

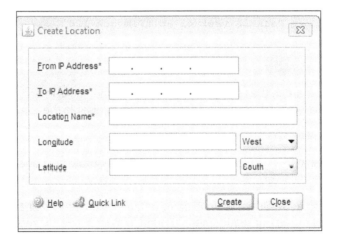

The setup entails a main site that processes traffic all the time and a disaster recovery site that comes up when the main site goes down. The entire GSLB algorithm is DNS-based. The GSLB configuration can be used for the following:

- ▸ Disaster recovery
- ▸ Load sharing
- ▸ Proximity/performance

The Citrix NetScaler **Metric Exchange Protocol** (**MEP**) is a channel of communication between NetScaler devices across various geographical locations; it works on TCP port 3011 and, to be secure, port 3009. It is a NetScaler proprietary protocol and is used in GSLB to monitor the health of the sites. There are also the typical monitors that are bound to the load LB vserver.

With MEP and monitors enabled, the health of the remote sites can be measured from the monitors. But if monitors are not enabled, then the health of the site is measured with the help of MEP. The CLI command to enable MEP is as follows:

```
root@ns>set gslb site Packtsite -metricExchange  ?
  ENABLED
  DISABLED
```

The site metrics, the network metrics, and persistence information are shared between the GSLB sites only if the MEP is enabled. An important note is to check if the feature is enabled before you get started with the GSLB configuration. If you are going with the static proximity type of GSLB, then you would need to load the location database on the NetScaler device. To verify whether the database is properly loaded, issue the `show locationparameter` command and check the current static entries. If the incoming traffic does not match any entry in the location database, then the request is processed using the round robin method.

How to do it...

We will focus on a few case studies, most commonly seen in GSLB.

Case 1: The three critical aspects for GSLB are the Gslb site, Gslb vserver, and Gslb service. The site address references NetScaler at each location. These three aspects are interlinked to make it easier for the traffic to be sent to the right location.

For example, there are two sites in this recipe, main and DR. You will have to repeat the configuration on both the devices:

1. **Domain**: `www.packttest.com`
   - ❑ **ADNS servers**: `172.16.1.6` for the main and DR sites
   - ❑ **Vservers**: `172.16.32.24` for the main site and `172.16.32.114` for the DR site
   - ❑ **Site addresses**: `171.12.12.33` for the main site and `171.12.12.3` for the DR site

2. Configure the gslb sites as follows:
   ```
   add gslb site gslb_local 171.12.12.33 -publicIP 171.12.12.33
   add gslb site gslb_remote 171.12.12.3-publicIP 171.12.12.3
   ```

3. Configure the gslb services: The gslb service might be a LB vserver or a direct third-party server:

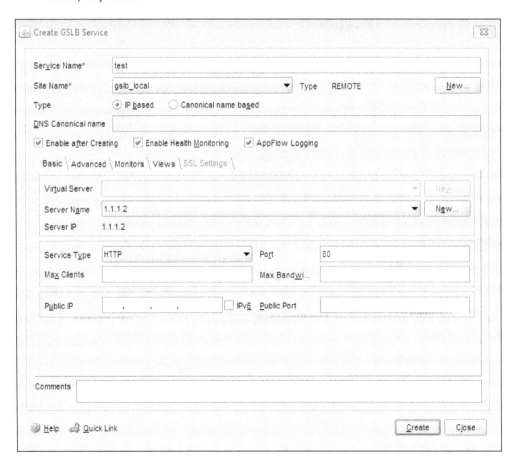

4. Configure the gslb vserver and bind the services to the vserver:

```
add gslb vserver packtmain_gslb_vserver HTTP
add gslb vserver packtdr_gslb_vserver HTTP
bind gslb vserver packtmain_gslb_vserver -serviceName test
bind gslb vserver packtdr_gslb_vserver -serviceName test_dr
```

5. An important configuration is setting the backup vserver under the **Advanced** tab:

```
set gslb vserver packtmain_gslb_vserver -backupVServer packtdr_
gslb_vserver
```

6. Bind the domain to the gslb vserver as follows:

```
bind gslb vserver packtmain_gslb_vserver -domainName www.
packttest.com -TTL 5
```

7. Last but not the least, the ADNS service should be configured in NetScaler in such a way that NS would become authoritative for the domain www.packttest.com. The CLI command to configure NetScaler as an ADNS service is as follows:

```
>add service main_site_adns_server 172.16.1.6 ADNS 53
```

The IP address that is used here can be a MIP or SNIP address.

Case 2: The previous section shows the basic GSLB setup. In this case study, we will see the **Dynamic proximity** process, where NetScaler chooses the site that has the least **Round trip time** (**RTT**). For the first time alone, NetScaler chooses a site using the round robin method and then begins its RTT calculation using the following three steps in the same order sequentially:

1. ICMP
2. DNS
3. TCP

In the event that ICMP is blocked mid-way before reaching the site (anywhere on the Internet), it uses the second method listed (that is, DNS query), and finally a TCP handshake is used for the RTT calculation if the DNS query also does not give a response. This procedure is depicted in the next screenshot.

The RTT table can be viewed in the **Configuration Utility** tab under **GSLB | LDNS Entries**. If **RTT** shows as **0**, then the time taken is less than one millisecond and if RTT shows as **T-out** then it indicates that the destination is unreachable. If all three preceding methods fail, it will take the backup LB method configured.

We can also use the static location database that maps the IP address range to the location area. This database is then loaded on the appliance. When the client's LDNS requests the site IP address from NetScaler, which acts as the ADNS, NetScaler parses through this location database to determine the location of the client's LDNS IP address, and then sends the nearest site IP address to the client. This method is called **Static Proximity**:

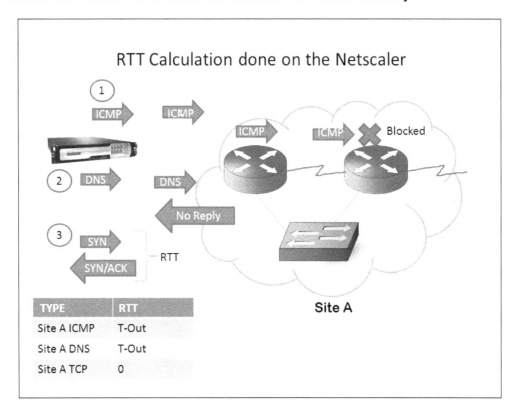

TYPE	RTT
Site A ICMP	T-Out
Site A DNS	T-Out
Site A TCP	0

The CLI command to configure dynamic proximity is as follows:

```
>set gslb vserver packtGSLB -lbMethod MethodType
>set gslb vserver packtGSLB -lbMethod RTT
```

The RTT is calculated between the LDNS of the client and the site IP address.

How it works...

In both the case studies, NetScaler first receives the DNS request in case it is acting as the ADNS for that particular domain, and according to the LB algorithm set, it directs the response either to itself or another NetScaler situated in a different geographical location. In this recipe, since we are only focusing on disaster recovery, the main site will continue to process traffic until it goes down.

The GSLB local and remote site is used for the **Metric Exchange Protocol** (**MEP**) communication to share the status and health of the sites. When configuring sites on NetScaler, there is an option for the public IP address. This can be left blank if there is no firewall in the picture that does any NAT translation.

To check if the configuration is accurate, run the following command:

```
root@ns# host www.packttest.com 172.16.1.6
```

The output will be similar to the following:

```
Using domain server:
Name: 172.16.1.6
Address: 172.16.1.6#53
```

The aliases are:

```
www.domain.com has address 171.12.12.33.
```

The following image shows the flow of GSLB at its basic level:

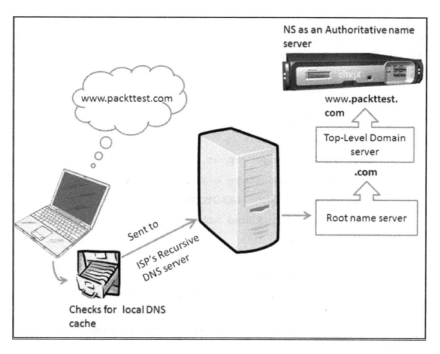

There's more...

This section concentrates on tidbits and troubleshooting techniques:

Tips and troubleshooting:

1. Run the following CLI command to check the GSLB sites:

```
root@NS> show gslb site
        1)        packtsiteA (10.xx.xx.xx)          Site Type: REMOTE

          Metric exchange: ENABLED        Metric exchange
status:        ACTIVE  Public IP: 10.xx.xx.xx
          Network metric exchange: ENABLED          Persistence
session        exchange: ENABLED
          Trigger Monitors: ALWAYS
        2)        packtsiteA (10.xx.xx.xx)  Site Type: LOCAL
          Metric exchange: ENABLED        Public IP: 10.xx.xx.xx


------OUTPUT SNIPPED------
```

From the preceding output, we can see that NetScaler configured for GSLB will have one local and one or many remote sites (NetScalers in different data center locations).

2. Check for the GSLB vserver as follows:

```
root@NS> show gslb vservers
1)        packtvserver - HTTP        State: UP
          Last state change was at XXXXXXXXXXXXXX (x ms)
          Time since last state change: 0 days, xx:xx:xx.xx
          Configured Method: LEASTCONNECTION
          Current Method: Round Robin, Reason:  Bound service's
state changed to UP
          No. of Bound Services :  1 (Total)        1 (Active)
          Persistence: NONE
          Disable Primary Vserver on Down: DISABLED        Site
Persistence: NONE
          Backup: packt_gslb_vserver Backup Session Timeout: 0
----OUTPUT SNIPPED----------
```

The preceding output shows the gslb vserver, where the domain name for the site is configured and the gslb services are bound.

3. Check for GSLB services as follows:

    ```
    root@ns> show gslb service
    1)          packtsvc (10.xx.xx.xx: 80)- HTTP      Server:     10.xx.xxx.
    xx          State: UP
                Effective State: UP
                Max Conn: 0                   Max Bandwidth: 0 kbits
                PublicIP: 10.xx.xxx.xx PublicPort: 80
                Type: REMOTE                  Site Name: packtsiteA
                Client IP: DISABLED
                Down state flush: ENABLED
                Site Persistence: NONE
                Threshold: BELOW
    ```

The preceding output shows the target LB or CS vserver and the LB method configured. NetScaler can be configured with a local and many remote GSLB services.

DOS and attack preventions (Should know)

Zero window, SSL renegotiation attacks, and so on, can be prevented using NetScaler. Even with simple ACLs, Citrix NetScaler has the ability to use ACLs on the fly for every new ACL added and need not wait for new sessions to trigger the ACL.

NetScaler provides end-to-end web security along with the **APP Firewall** module; the module can be used as a standalone or be integrated with NetScaler, and be used along with all the other features.

Getting ready

Half-open TCP SYN connections are what constitute a DOS attack. A half-open TCP connection (as shown in next image) is a state wherein it is stuck before the three-way handshake is completed (SYN-SYN/ACK-ACK). NetScaler defends such attacks by not allocating any memory for all the SYN requests hitting NetScaler. Instead, it sends a cookie to each client that requests the connection and allocates memory only after the FINAL ACK message containing the same cookie is received. While NS uses this mechanism of inserting cookies into the new TCP connections, the old ones are not interrupted.

This DOS attack prevention does not need anything to be explicitly enabled:

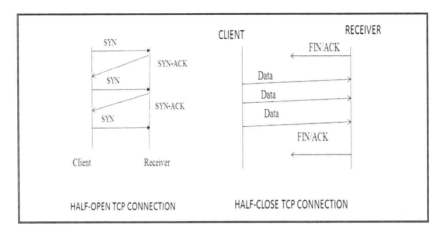

Brute force, slow post, and zero window attacks can be stopped on NetScaler with the help of the **rate-limiting** feature. Priority queuing can also be used to defend against DOS attacks:

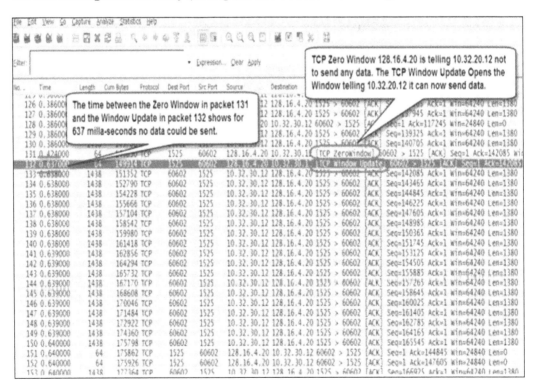

The preceding screenshot shows the zero-window packet in wireshark and legitimate clients in cases where the receive buffer is full and will send zero-window packets to the sender. How does NetScaler differentiate between a legit and an attack? This depends upon the number of concurrent small-window connections at a time and also on the MSS size (DDOS). The defense mechanism kicks in when the number of concurrent small-window connections are more than the number configured. If the attack has less than the number of simultaneous connections configured, then there is the zombie cleanup that kicks in when the connections move to the re-use pool.

These attacks can be found out even by polling with the following MIBs:

- `httpErrIncompleteRequests`
  `(1.3.6.1.4.1.5951.4.1.1.48.57)`
- `httpErrIncompleteHeaders`
  `(1.3.6.1.4.1.5951.4.1.1.48.60)`
- `tcpEStatsPerfZeroRwinRcvd`
  `(1.3.6.1.2.1.156.1.1.3.1.28)`

How to do it...

1. TCP/UDP flood protection is enabled by default; however, the HTTP DOS protection feature has to be enabled and policies have to be defined if you need it customized. To enable the HTTP DOS feature, use the following:

   ```
   root@ns>enable ns feature HttpDoSProtection
   root@ns> add dos policy httpdospol -DoS  -qDepth 30
   ```

   This policy can be bound to any HTTP services that need protection. While configuring the services, Max Client and Max Request should be set to confine the number of client connections to the Vserver and the number of requests on one persistent connection to the backend server.

2. Simple and Extended ACLs:

   The packet flow would begin with simple ACL (if configured) and then move on to extended ACLs. The ACL action can be ALLOW, DENY, and BRIDGE. The final action is bridging the packet without processing it. The implicit action of NetScaler, if it does not find any matching IP address, is to process the packet normally; when the ACL misses it, the counter would increment.

   - **Simple ACL**:
     ```
     add ns simpleacl  packtacl DENY -srcIP  10.122.23.40
     -destPort 1494 -protocol TCP
     ```

❑ **Extended ACL**:

```
add ns acl extpacktacl  DENY -srcport 80-1024 -destIP
192.168.1.1 -protocol TCP
```

 There are many further options such as `source mac`, `interface vlan`, and so on.

The traffic that hits the ACLs can be logged with the `[-logState option ENABLED]` command.

There is also an option to flush existing established connections after new ACLs are configured:

```
root@ns>flush simpleacl -estSessions
```

3. Rate-limiting can be done based on certain URL or client SRC IP addresses. Care must be taken to avoid mixing attacks with connections that come from behind a single IP address (that is, a proxy). To reduce any false positives, we can configure both `Client.IP` and `HTTP REQ` in the limit identifier. `threshold` specifies the number of requests before the defense mechanism kicks in.

```
root@ns>add ns limitSelector httpdos_limit_sel client.ip.SRC
```

```
root@ns>add ns limitIdentifier httpdos_limit_ident -threshold
1000 -timeSlice 120000 -mode REQUEST_RATE -limitType SMOOTH
-selectorName httpdos_limit_sel
```

This configuration can be fine-tuned more by setting the action that NetScaler takes for the DOS attack:

```
root@ns> add responder policy httpdospol "HTTP.REQ.URL.CONTAINS("www.
packttest.com") && SYS.CHECK_LIMIT(\"httpdos_limit_ident\")" RESET
```

This responder policy can be bound globally. According to this policy, NetScaler would reset all the connections that come within the time interval. This reset action can also be changed to log a message to the user that says the limit has been reached and try again later:

```
root@ns>add responder action dos_act respondwith "\"Exceeded the maximum
number of retries\r\n\r\n\""
```

How it works...

Priority queuing of NetScaler helps in defending against DOS attacks by prioritizing the traffic hitting NetScaler; this can be done by filtering the traffic according to certain criteria and then prioritizing it. At a maximum, three priority queuing policies can be bound to a load-balancing Vserver. While configuring priority queuing, the priority, threshold, and weight needs to be specified along with an implicit action.

Each priority queuing policy can be set based on priority and weight:

```
>add pq policy packtPQpol -rule HTTP.REQ.URL.CONTAINS("/networktest")
-priority 1 -weight 30 [-qDepth <positive_integer> | -polqDepth
<positive_integer>]
```

This policy will filter traffic based on URLs that contain `networktest`, give it `priority 1`, and assign a weight of `30`. Weight should be set for efficient functioning, because without weights only the higher priority requests will continue getting served and the lower priority requests will be kept on the back burner. To avoid this situation, we go for weighted queuing where, for example, the three important departments in an organization—Engineering, IT, and Finance—can be configured as follows for serving traffic with priority queuing:

```
Engineering: Priority 1-Weight 30
IT             : Priority 2-Weight 20
Finance        : Priority 3-Weight 10
```

From this configuration, after 30 requests have been served in Engineering, the packet flow will move on to serve 20 requests of IT, and so on in a cycle. This way, the Finance department is not completely ignored until there is nothing to serve for Engineering and IT.

From the preceding CLI command, we see an option to specify either queue depth or policy queue depth; the difference between the two is that the first option specifies the value of the total number of requests waiting to hit a particular vserver to which the policy is bound, and the latter specifies the total number of waiting clients belonging to the policy.

The HTTP DOS policies are also configured with something called `qdepth` and client detect rate. The queue depth, as mentioned before, would be the maximum number of connections placed in the surge queue at a time and the client detect rate would be the percentage of traffic before which the HTTP DOS policy should be applied.

 While setting `qDepth` for HTTP DOS, care should be taken to see that the `qdepth` value is more than the window size.

Even for the client detect rate option, please note that an optimum percentage should be chosen for sending the JavaScript challenge responses. If the percentage is too high, it would flood the upstream routers or switches.

There's more...

Distributed denial-of-service (DDOS) attack gets past the initial stages of defense, because it sends the complete HTTP header intact with all the information necessary to the server and then slows down, sending a few bytes per few seconds. Priority queuing can help in avoiding these attacks.

Before implementing any DOS protection, it is safe to monitor the traffic characteristics and so on. Also, instead of just enabling the DOS protection feature, and so on, and leaving it at default, it is recommended to fine-tune the setting according to your network topology.

Learning Application Firewall (Must know)

The AppFw module checks the HTTP host and referrer headers that are present in the requests, and prevents any attacks to modify the content of forms sent to the server. It also maintains the state of each session with the help of its own session cookies. This section would help us dive into the possible features available in APPFw. Citrix NetScaler App Firewall is compliant with the PCI-DSS criteria; it also protects zero-day or custom-made attacks, which we will see in detail later in this chapter

Getting ready

We had a pre-sequel to the attack prevention in the previous recipe, touching only on the first line of defense; in this recipe we will discuss the app firewall module in a little more detail.

In the Configuration Utility, there is a checkbox for learning. Hence, before you set the box to production, you need to first gather a sample of the actual traffic hitting NetScaler and then enable blocking.

The HTTP referer headers are used to denote the previous page they were sourced from, and this can be exploited to get access to websites by masquerading as though coming from a valid website—it is similar to spoofing. In the App Firewall module, there is a feature called **Start URL**, where we can validate the referer header, if present. As shown in the following screenshot, **Block**, **Learn**, **Log**, and **Stat** are the actions that can be configured against each of the features.

There are two types of profiles that can be configured on the APP Firewall:

- Basic
- Advanced

The difference between the two of them is that the **Learn** checks will not be enabled by default in the basic profile. Since the security checks all operations on the HTTP responses, it requires resources to retain and compare the information it sent previously to the users:

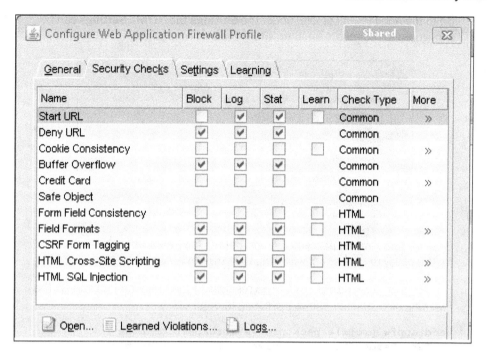

Learned Violations can be seen and altered according to the organization's requirements as shown in the preceding screenshot. Starting with NetScaler version 10, using the **CEF** (**Common Event Format**) logs, one can decide whether to deploy by clicking on **Logs...** or not.

Also in a high-availability setup, the learned data can be propagated to the secondary device, so it would help in a seamless failover (only on NetScaler version 10).

How to do it...

In this section, we are going to see how **Start URL** and the Cross Site scripting prevention work with NetScaler App Firewall:

1. Configure App Firewall profile to be basic, and configure a policy with RULE (here we are going to use `HTTP.REQ.IS_VALID`), which means anything and everything.

2. Tick the **Learning** checkbox of **Start URL** before you enable blocking.

3. Go to the App Firewall profile, under the **Settings** tab. **HTML Settings** can be configured to redirect to another URL or load an html page:

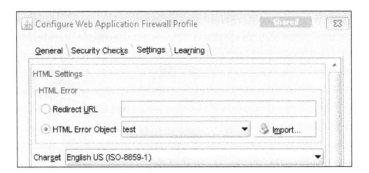

4. Bind the App Firewall policy to the appropriate **load balancing** (**LB** Vserver, for the policy to take effect when the user tries to access the LB Vserver.

   For example, `www.packttest.com` resolves to the VIP of an LB Vserver. The following code snippet shows the config through CLI:

```
>add appfw profile packtpro -startURLAction none
-RefererHeaderCheck if_present -CSRFtagAction block
log stats -crossSiteScriptingAction learn log stats
-crossSiteScriptingCheckCompleteURLs ON -XMLSQLInjectionAction
none -XMLXSSAction none -XMLWSIAction none -XMLValidationAction
none -useHTMLErrorObject ON -HTMLErrorObject test

>add appfw policy packtpol HTTP.REQ.IS_VALID packtpro

>bind lb vserver packtlb packt_svc

>bind lb vserver packtlb -policyName packtpol -priority 100
-gotoPriorityExpression END -type REQUEST
```

Under the **Learning** Tab of the App Firewall profile, clicking on **Start URL** will show us the list of scripts it has learned from the traffic hitting the NetScaler:

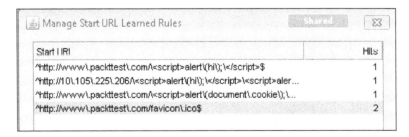

With this data, we can select what is needed to be deployed. Once deployed, it creates a white list of URLs, which are obtained from all the responses during the user session. This functionality is called the URL closure and can be enabled under the **Start URL** feature (Go to the **Security Checks** tab of the App Firewall profile):

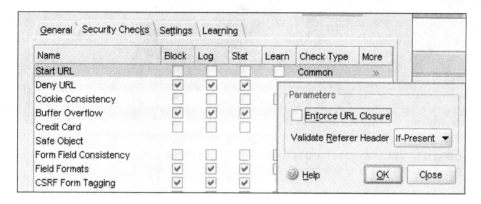

A simple setup is used to demonstrate the **Start URL** protection as shown in the preceding screenshot.

This protection can be tested by creating a query in the URL, for example, `http://www.packttest.com`, which is an LB VIP created with Netscaler. This URL is listed in the white list with the **Start URL** feature; however, `http://www.packttest.com/?<script>alert(hi)</script>` is not, and should be blocked as this is injecting a script along with the URL. To test this feature, we need to enable the **Block** checkbox in the **Security Checks** tab of the profile.

We could see the protection happening from the `ns.log`, after accessing the preceding URL:

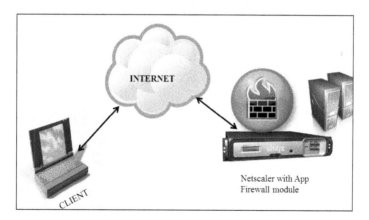

When there is a violation of the rules, it is logged in the NetScaler BSD shell under `/var/log/ns.log`:

```
Oct 14 17:26:29 <local0.info> 10.105.225.207 10/14/2012:17:26:29 GMT   PPE-0 : AP
PFW APPFW_CSRF_TAG 1803 :   10.65.78.216 1336-PPE0 LFocMi/Ux5yLQUrQGrCPIeM562IAOO
D packtpro http://www.packttest.com/●●●●_●●●●_●●●●_●●●●●●.xml?&lt;script&g
t;%20alert(hi)&lt;/script&gt; CSRF Tag validation failed: <blocked>
Oct 14 17:26:54 <local0.info> 10.105.225.207 10/14/2012:17:26:54 GMT   PPE-0 : UI
 CMD_EXECUTED 1804 :   User nsroot - Remote_ip 10.65.78.216 - Command "login" - S
tatus "Success"
Oct 14 17:27:01 <local0.info> 10.105.225.207 10/14/2012:17:27:01 GMT   PPE-0 : UI
 CMD_EXECUTED 1805 :   User nsroot - Remote_ip 10.65.78.216 - Command "shell" - S
tatus "Success"
]
```

Here, along with the timestamp, we can see the URL being accessed as well as the `<blocked>` action taken by the App Firewall.

After learning and deploying a certain rule, we can see the rule in the running config:

```
>show run | grep packtpro
bind appfw profile packtpro -startURL "^http://www\\.packttest\\.com/$"
```

The second part of the testing is to check whether the same profile works with a CSRF attack.

The **CSRF** (**Cross-Site Request Forgery**) attacks work on logged-in user sessions, modifying the HTTP request. NetScaler adds a unique token to the forms that are sent to the users and validate the token on subsequent requests and responses between client and server.

The same setup and configuration used in the preceding demo is used here. We are going to test the site by using any link or URL on the webpage and add a script or query to the link while accessing, for example, the same VIP as used before, `http://www.packttest.com`, which opens up the web page, clicking on a link or URL on the web page `http://www.packttest.com/citrix_products_netscaler.html?<script>alert(hi)</script>`.

As we can see in the following screenshot, the `ns.log` has a log message stating that the packet is blocked due to a tag validation failure:

```
Oct 13 23:56:04 <local0.info> 10.105.225.207 10/13/2012:23:56:04 GMT  PPE-0 : UI
 CMD_EXECUTED 1370 :  User nsroot - Remote_ip 10.65.79.203 - Command "show ns co
nfig" - Status "Success"
Oct 13 23:56:43 <local0.info> 10.105.225.207 10/13/2012:23:56:43 GMT  PPE-0 : AP
PFW APPFW_STARTURL 1371 :  10.65.79.203 1070-PPE0 oryd463TX/1SZcs/KLHluldRW2IA00
0 packtpro Disallow Illegal URL: http://www.packttest.com/&lt;script&gt;alert(hi
);&lt;/script&gt; <blocked>
Oct 13 23:57:37 <local0.info> 10.105.225.207 10/13/2012:23:57:37 GMT  PPE-0 : UI
 CMD_EXECUTED 1372 :  User nsroot - Remote_ip 10.65.79.203 - Command "sftp-serve
r" - Status "Success"
```

As always, it also displays the URL that is being accessed (outlined in the preceding screenshot).

Here is a HTTP header trace to show the transactions between NetScaler and the client:

```
GET /Test.xml?<script>alert(hi)</script> HTTP/1.1
Accept: application/x-ms-application, image/jpeg, application/
xaml+xml, image/gif, image/pjpeg, application/x-ms-xbap, application/
x-shockwave-flash, application/vnd.ms-excel, application/vnd.ms-
powerpoint, application/msword, */*
Accept-Language: en-US
User-Agent: Mozilla/4.0 (compatible; MSIE 8.0; Windows NT 6.1; WOW64;
Trident/4.0; SLCC2; .NET CLR 2.0.50727; .NET CLR 3.5.30729; .NET CLR
3.0.30729; Media Center PC 6.0; InfoPath.3)
Accept-Encoding: gzip, deflate
Host: www.packttest.com
Connection: Keep-Alive
Cookie: citrix_ns_id=SQIoGifoC0oF+GaOVYl3cCJDKTQA000

HTTP/1.1 200 OK
Pragma: "no-cache"
Content-Length: 99
Connection: close
<html>
<head>
    <title>THIS PAGE IS BLOCKED BY CITRIX APPLICAITON FIREWALL
  </title>
 </head>
</html>
```

As we can see in the preceding header, the session is already established and hence we see the cookie in the GET request of the client containing citrix_ns_id=SQIoGifoC0oF+GaO VY13cCJDKTQA000.

NetScaler gracefully terminates the connection with a 200 OK message, as can be seen from a wireshark capture taken on NetScaler (see the following screenshot). The FIN and PUSH flags are highlighted in the screenshot.

There are other functionalities, such as masking the credit card numbers and other safe objects while sending responses to the users. The safe objects are configurable on NetScaler, such that when traffic hits the NetScaler, the App Firewall module checks for any safe object pattern in the requests and responses:

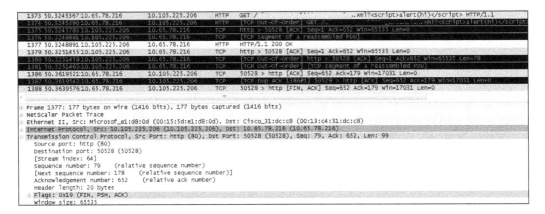

Role-based access control

Role-based access control is a feature that is used to control the admin access rights to NetScaler. We can configure the command policy to add/remove commands, show commands or restrict commands, to users. A predefined command policy is shown in the following screenshot:

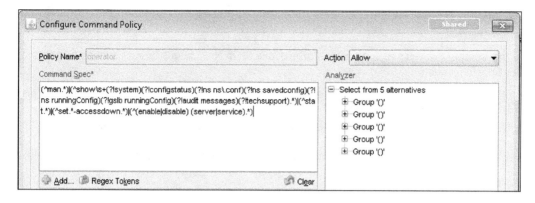

The CLI command to configure a test user:

```
CLI>add system cmdPolicy test ALLOW "(^\\S+\\s+serviceGroup.*)|(^\\S+\\
s+vserver.*)"
```

How it works...

The Citrix App Firewall module comes in at both the request- and response-side processing of traffic. After the content switching or LB vserver (whichever is configured as client facing), the App Firewall module parses through the packets to check for anomalies. Similarly at the response side after SSL decryption, rewrite (if any) content filtering and then App Firewall before sending the response to the client.

In the *How to do it...* section of this recipe, we saw the configuration setting for defense against **Start URL** and CSRF attacks. The AppFw first learns the URLs passing through it using the **Learning** module before we deploy the rules according to our requirement. We would be able to see the rules learnt by the AppFw in the Managed Learned Rules.

In the *Role-based access control* section, we saw how to control the management access of NetScaler for different users at different levels. We would be able to restrict them based on read-only commands, read/write commands, superuser commands, and so on.

App Firewall needs to be used with utmost planning as it is resource intensive. In sites where Integrated Caching and App firewall is used, CPU usage will tend to be on the higher side. All NetScaler MPX series that have 4 GB of RAM are capable of handling both caching and App Firewall implementation. Typically, the Application Firewall sits in front of the caching module and the best part about this is it does not require remodeling one's network; instead it is similar to adding on the existing network, making it more secure.

There's more...

In this section, we will see the new features available in NetScaler's latest versions and also a few known issues.

Tips and troubleshooting

A few commands that will help us in troubleshooting the App Firewall issues are as follows:

- `show appfw stats`: This output shows the request and response rate per second, the violation stats, and the number of server-side response error pages (for example, starting with `4xx` and `5xx`).

- `show appfw settings`:

  ```
  DefaultProfile:  APPFW_BYPASS UndefAction:  APPFW_BLOCK
  SessionTimeout:  900      SessionLifetime:  0
  SessionCookieName:  citrix_ns_id ImportSizeLimit:  134217728
  CookiePostEncryptPrefix:  ENC
  Done
  ```

  As the output denotes, this displays the default profile and action. The default session timeout (in seconds), beyond which the App Firewall module will terminate the idle user session, the cookie name, and so on, are all configurable.

- `/var/log/ns.log` and `messages.gz`: These commands will show the App Firewall logs in addition to the packet captures, and so on.

Starting with NetScaler version 10, the Common Event Format logging is enabled on NetScaler. In fact, the logs contain the source port in addition with the IP address and the HTTP method used by the client/users, which is very useful for debugging purposes.

Importing and exporting the App Firewall profile configuration across NetScaler devices makes it easier for the administrator to configure on many NetScaler appliances in one go.

Sessionless URL closure has the same functionality as session URL closure, with the only difference being that instead of tracking a session based on a cookie, the App Firewall module now inserts token into the responses that are being sent to the client.

 Once deployed in the main production site, it is no longer required to enable **Learning** for each of the subfeatures in an AppFw profile, since that would only cause more and more resources to get depleted.

The Application Firewall, though deployed in a Layer 3/Layer 4 setup, works mainly on Layer 7 HTTP. It is recommended to test this feature in your labs before making it sit directly on your production environment, even though the configuration is as simple as ticking a checkbox and enabling a few options. The results should be optimal for your organization's standpoint.

The Access Gateway integration for Citrix XenApp and XenDesktop (Become an expert)

This section guides you through implementing Access Gateway with XenApp or XenDesktop. The AGEE appliance is used to establish SSL VPN in many modes, such as clientless and full-client VPN.

The Access Gateway Enterprise VPX Edition is a stripped-down version of NetScaler that will help provide VPN access to XA/XD.

ICA is a Citrix proprietary protocol for application server systems; it works at Layer 6 (presentation layer). It uses TCP port 1494 to establish connections, and the server responds with a dynamically allocated port (in the case of a session reliability being used, the port would change to 2598.)

Session reliability is for keeping the session alive when there is loss of connectivity. ICA has keepalives that work exactly like TCP keepalives, except that they work on Layer 6 and are not enabled by default. ICA keepalives are used when session reliability is not enabled.

Getting ready

Basic versus smart access: these are the two modes provided by Access Gateway to the users. The difference between the two modes is that basic has unlimited ICA connections and only a platform license is required; for smart access, both Platform and universal licenses are needed. The smart access mode allows full VPN connectivity, EPA, clientless VPN, and so on, while using Citrix Receiver to access the applications through the VPN.

AGEE acts as an ICA proxy for XenApp and XenDesktop; it seals the traffic with HTTPS before it is sent to the client. Only full SSL certificates signed by a trusted **certificate authority** (**CA**) are required by the AGEE Vserver for the VPN to work; self-signed certificates cannot be used.

EPA (**endpoint analyses**) scans can be configured on the Access Gateway to implement security on hosted desktops and applications, and user access can be controlled based on this.

How to do it...

Consider the cases discussed in this section:

Case 1

First we are going to set up the VPN in basic mode access:

1. Set up an AGEE Vserver, bind the appropriate SSL certificate to it, and select the access mode as basic.

   SSL is the only protocol available while configuring the AGEE Vserver.

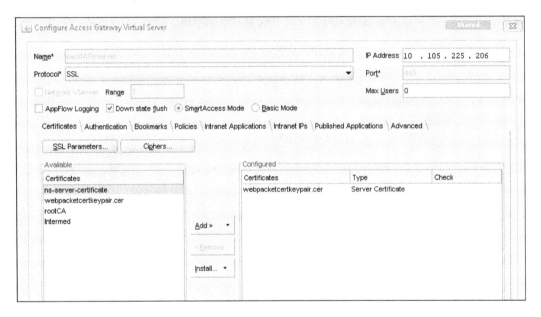

If there is a root and intermediate certificate for the server certificate obtained, they also need to be loaded onto the box and linked to each other.

The following screenshot shows the server certificate linked with the intermediate root CA, which in turn is linked to the root CA certificate:

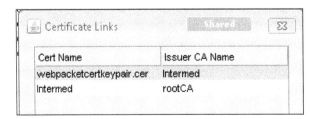

2. Configure bookmarks and FTP share links to local intranet sites and applications.

3. Under **Access Gateway**, go to **Global Settings**.

   There will be four tabs namely **Network Configuration, Security, Client Experience,** and **Published Applications**.

   Under **Network Configurations**, there is an option to set the DNS IP, which enables you to use any internal FQDN, and advanced options on the same tab let you configure how to use **IIPs** (**Intranet IPs**), and so on.

   The **Security** tab has a default operation, **ALLOW/DENY,** that can be set, and advanced options where we can restrict the users based on EPA scans and policies.

   Under the **Client Experience** tab, options such as **SplitTunnel** (which has two options, **ON** or **OFF**, that define whether the traffic from the client should completely go through the tunnel or use both the VPN tunnel and local inter-network), **Session,** and **Client idle timeout**, and an option to specify a homepage (optional) are available. Single sign-on to web applications and client cleanup prompt (prompts when logging out of VPN) are also available.

   Published Applications are also available to set ICA proxy to **ON** or **OFF** and to set the web interface link address. The ICA proxy settings come into the picture, when deciding between full, clientless, and full-client VPN.

4. Access the fully qualified doman name (FQDN) specified in the certificate, using HTTPS, and make sure you do not get the security warning. If you do get, please check if the certificates are loaded in your local machine along with the intermediate certificate, if any (Go to **Start | Run** and type mmc). After loading the certificates, please verify that the certificates can be seen under **Tools | Internet Options | Content | Certificates**.

An intranet IP (IIP) pool can be configured, if you require the client connecting with only the range of IP addresses specified:

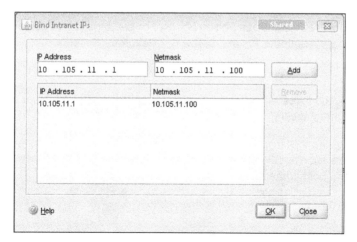

This IIP pool can be set in **Global Settings** or under **AGEE Vserver | Intranet IPs**. The preceding screenshot shows the Intranet IP configuration and the following screenshot shows the **Global Settings** page. The Intranet IP is used to assign IP address to the users connecting to the VPN. If the range of IP addresses is exhausted by the users, either an IP address can be reclaimed from a user who is in a logged off state or there is a setting that allows MIP to be used as IIP when no other address is available:

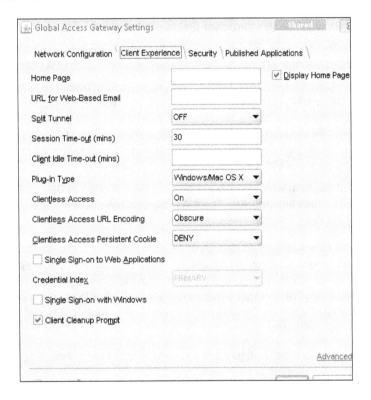

So, instead of global settings, if customized per user or per application, we can configure session profile and policy under **Access Gateway | Policies | Session**.

Case 2

In this case study, the focus will be on customizing the VPN configuration per user group, in turn making it more secure.

First we will set up the VPN in smart mode access. Smart Access is used for advanced VPN configurations such as EPA scans, access to XenApp using web interface, and pre-authentication and post-authentication scans.

We will be seeing how to configure each in this section.

Smart Access provides Full VPN connectivity and to enable that we need to set the ICA **proxy** and **Clientless Access** options to **OFF** for full VPN. There is also the possibility of setting the VPN to full for certain users and clientless for the rest or vice versa, using session policies.

Session policies can be configured by using regular expressions, as you would configure any other policies on NetScaler. Session policies can be configured based on the users:

- ▸ Network subnet (network based)
- ▸ The version of the antivirus software running on the client machine
- ▸ The set of processes that is required to be running/existing for the VPN to work (client security)
- ▸ Client's connection type/speed (client security)
- ▸ Client certificate scan (general)
- ▸ Hard disk encryption and even date and time

The session policy configuration can be anywhere between simple expressions such as `URL = ="/*.asp"` or `HTTP.REQ.URL.CONTAINS"/mycompany"` and compound expressions such as `"CLIENT.APPLICATION.PROCESS (notepad.exe).EXISTS"`.

Session policies can be bound globally, at the vserver level or the user level, and the preference works from the user level to groups to the vserver and finally to the global level. These policies are evaluated after the client is authenticated as it is more towards the client connection settings and so on.

The next step towards setting up smart access is traffic policy. Traffic policy is used to configure the file type associations for hosted applications on XenApp or XenDesktop.

File type associations help users in editing any document on the server itself instead of downloading it to the client and changing it. Traffic policies can be created for this, however, only with HTTP as protocol.

The session and traffic policies, after their creation, are bound at the vserver level:

```
add vpn url test test "http://10.105.225.201"

add vpn intranetApplication Remote-Desktop TCP 10.105.225.216 -destPort
3389 -interception PROXY -srcIP 127.0.0.1 -srcPort 3389

add vpn intranetApplication Test-1.1.1.1 ANY 1.1.1.1 -destPort 1-65535
-interception TRANSPARENT

add vpn vserver packtAGvserver SSL 10.105.225.206 443 -appflowLog
DISABLED

add vpn sessionAction testpro -splitTunnel ON -defaultAuthorizationAction
ALLOW -SSO ON -clientlessVpnMode OFF -clientlessModeUrlEncoding
TRANSPARENT -clientlessPersistentCookie ALLOW
```

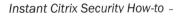

EPA scans can also be configured as a part of the pre-authentication policy and bound to the vserver, thereby letting the CAG scan the client before sending the authentication request.

In the case of configuring pre-authentication policy, checks related to the client's registry values, and so on, can be done. A sample config is as follows:

```
CLIENT.REG(HKEY_LOCAL_MACHINE\\Software\\Symantec\\Norton\
AntiVirus_Version).EXISTS
```

Whenever an EPA scan takes place, an EPA plugin is downloaded to the client to scan according to the policy set on the CAG.

The benefit of EPA, as we can see, is that users can connect from anywhere while still maintaining the internal network risk free.

Traffic policies as discussed earlier are used to configure the file type associations, and for implementing that we require the Citrix XenApp plugin. Once the traffic policy is bound to the AGEE Vserver, each of the file extensions in the published application's (that is, on the presentation server) content redirection properties should be enabled.

Another point to be noted is, if there are any routes that need to be loaded onto the client who is connecting to the VPN for accessing any intranet network, the intranet applications are configured for that particular network/subnet.

Moving onto the web interface part of the configuration, the web interface link address can be specified under **Global Settings** or in the **Session** profile, and it can be bound to the vserver. The latter is preferred if a customized config is required. To integrate Access Gateway with the web interface, we will begin by configuring a default site PNAgent. The site should be configured for the Gateway Direct mode. You would also need to enter the FQDN of the URL that you want the users to hit.

For example, for `http://www.webpackt.com`, the FQDN would be `www.webpackt.com`.

While accessing through mobile devices, it is recommended not to enable session reliability (if unsure whether the mobile device has support for the feature or not). The last action item is to add the **STA** (**Secure Ticketing Authority**). The STA's main function is to generate a ticket for a session as well as to validate that ticket.

Now, let's discuss how to specify STA:

> ▸ When the ticket is generated and sent to the **web interface** (**WI**), the WI includes the STA ticket in the ICA file that is sent to the client. When this ICA session is launched, the STA validates the ticket. Refer to the following screenshot of applications and other options present in a full VPN client or XenApp plugin:

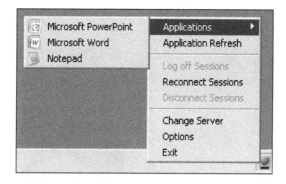

▸ This is used, if the server name is on a different port that should also be specified.

The following screenshot shows the STA config screen. As we can see in the following screenshot, the textbox where we add the URL has the format clearly given:

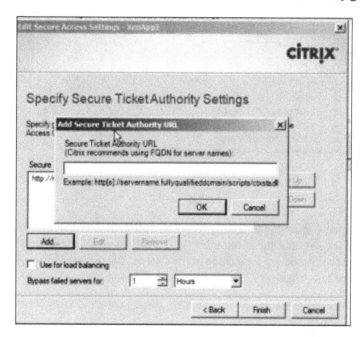

Once the STA is configured on web interface, it needs to be configured on the Access Gateway under **Vserver | Published Applications | Secure Ticket Authority-Add**.

How it works...

The following diagram shows the working of CAG in smart access mode:

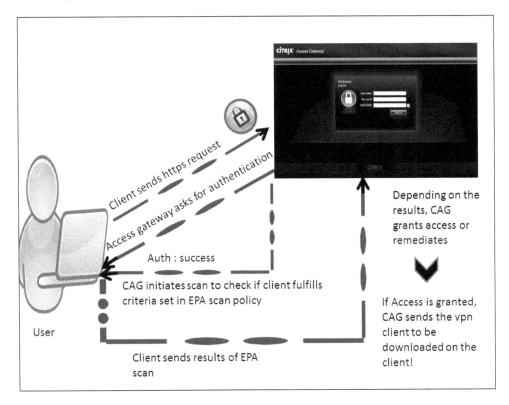

In smart access mode, after the authentication of the client, the Access Gateway will forward the authentication to the web interface (this is configurable during the site creating process, where you require the authentication to take place at the CAG or WI). The XenApp services' site that is created will appear to the user when he/she is met with all the eligibility criteria (scan).

How this works is briefly explained in the following steps:

1. Client sends the HTTPS request to the FQDN of the AGEE Vserver.

2. Authentication credentials are obtained from the user (either two-factor authentication or simple AD or OTP).

3. Once the client is authenticated, the CAG scans for the necessary processes or antivirus updates and so on that are available.

4. The results of the scans are sent to the CAG. After that, depending on what is configured as the action, the user is dropped or redirected to another site, during which the user can check what went wrong and rectify it (that is, if it is a valid user).

5. Once the access is granted, the VPN client is downloaded if full VPN is configured, or else the clientless VPN session gets established.

6. While launching any applications from the Citrix XenApp plugin or online plugin, the applications should always be in the `.ica` format.

> **Important note**
>
> While accessing VPN, the intranet portal gets appended at the end, for example, `https://www.webpackt.com/cvpn/http/packtlb.com`.
>
> To hide `http/packtlb.com`, we can use the rewrite or URL transformation feature.

There's more...

In this section, we will see a few tips and important points to remember while deploying Access Gateway Enterprise Edition.

Tips and troubleshooting

▸   Primarily, a lot of issues are based on the certificates that are bound to the AGEE Vserver.

▸   No self-signed certificate will work with AGEE.

▸   If there is more than one root CA certificate, the intermediates should be linked on both the NetScaler as well as the client machines.

▸   The STA URL configured on Access Gateway and the web interface should match, otherwise the STA servers will not come up.

▸   If STA URL is configured with FQDN, make sure the FQDN is resolvable on NetScaler before going ahead with the configuration; this is yet another cause for the STA servers not coming up.

▸   Whenever we configure bookmarks to be bound to the AGEE Vserver with clientless access configuration, there is a checkbox that says **Use Access Gateway as a reverse proxy**. When this checkbox is enabled, users go through the CAG to reach the website; however, if it is disabled, the connections go directly from client to the website.

▸   Check if the domain CA certificates are present in the web interface, if not, we would need to install them in the WI as well.

▸   The same STA servers can be configured across the XenApp farms.

▸   Do not forget to check **Trust requests sent to the XML service** and make sure only trusted services are used.

▸   Mobile users that use Citrix Receiver to connect can segregate the policies based on HTTP user-agent header.

Many improvisations such as multiple STA servers for load balancing, web interface being configured as an LB Vserver, and the LB Vserver being pointed at the **AGEE Published Application** tab are available. The AGEE login page is also customized to suit the needs of the organization; however, care should be taken to keep a backup of the files that are modified, and too much of customizations can also break the VPN connection.

Network management (Must know)

Managing a network is equally as compelling as security; Citrix provides its own **command center** (**CC**) as a monitoring and manageability solution. This recipe shows what monitoring can be done on the NetScaler alone as well as how CC helps with the (**simple network management protocol**) **SNMP** polling.

The CC is used to smartly manage the network when there are multiple NetScaler devices.

It is used to manage the Citrix NetScaler, Access Gateway and App Firewall devices. It is a software solution that sits on the Linux or Windows systems. It has its own database or can be pointed to any external database.

Listed here are the functions of the Citrix CC:

- ▶ Fault management
- ▶ SSL certificate
- ▶ Planned upgrade/downgrade of devices

Getting ready

Collecting events and faults of devices on a regular basis can be done with the help of the CC, although NetScaler also has a basic level monitoring applet from which we can view the connections per second under load balancing, content switching, and so on.

The ports that are needed to be open between the CC server and NetScaler are as follows:

- ▶ SNMP ports 161 and 162
- ▶ SSH and SFTP (that is, 22)
- ▶ If the GUI configuration utility and dashboard need to be accessed from the CC client, port 80 and 3010 need to be allowed
- ▶ When the CC server is installed, HTTPS is enabled by default
- ▶ HTTP communication between CC client and NetScaler is 9090

The discovery process of the CC as well as the event logs of a device is automatic.

How to do it...

In this section, we will start with monitoring done on NetScaler and continue further with how to enable discovery automatically in the command center.

On the Netscaler Configuration Utility, there are three tabs: **Configuration**, **Monitoring**, and **Reporting Dashboards**.

The SNMP part of the config on NetScaler is simple and straightforward:

1. Go to **System | SNMP**. The first step in SNMP is to configure a community name on NetScaler. The default community name is **"public"**. The version of SNMP configured should be the same on NetScaler and the SNMP manager.

2. The SNMP manager needs to be configured on NetScaler.

3. Necessary traps it is required to send can also be configured in the **Config** utility under **System | SNMP | Traps**:

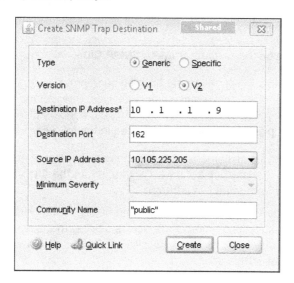

4. We can also classify traps by enabling the alarms to send logs with different severity such as **Critical**, **Warnings**, **Information**, and so on. The source IP address for sending these traps is by default the NetScaler IP, though it can be changed to MIP/SNIP (as per your configuration and firewall rules). NetScaler sends the trap messages to the configured trap destination and also to the logged-in /var/ns.log:

5. The MIBs for SNMP polling can be obtained from the **Downloads** tab of NetScaler Configuration Utility.

6. The SNMP OIDs of the vserver, services, or service groups that have been configured on the box can be found under **SNMP | SNMP OIDs**.

Now let's discuss the Citrix CC—an alternate Citrix solution provided at a much higher level and a Citrix standard for easily managing multiple devices. One can run the CC as a Windows discovery process. How you go about configuring it to automatically discover NetScaler, other Access Gateway and App firewall devices is discussed in the following steps:

1. Create a map by using name or network address. By creating a blank map, we can add devices to it at any point of time. For that, under the **Citrix Network** tab, navigate to **Maps | Add Name and Description**.

2. Configure NS pool by adding all the VIPs that belong to the NetScaler. This is used when implementing a common config across devices that change SSL certificates or upgrading, and so on. Under **Maps**, click on **Create a Netscaler pool** and add required devices to this pool.

The discovery process starts after adding the devices to the map. The discovery works based on hostname or IP address set in the map.

We can view the status of the discovery process in the CC under the **Citrix Network** tab. Click on the name of the map configured, and under the map, click on the **Discovery** status.

How it works...

The NetScaler MPX devices, such as 10500, 12500, and 15500, are rate limited per the license purchased, meaning there is a limit on the number of packets per seconds. SNMP traps can be configured to send a trap message when the threshold is exceeded.

The **Monitoring** tab of the NetScaler shows the number of connections, the number of TCP Est server connections, resource utilizations, and so on.

The following screenshot shows a sample screen showing the number of connections established for an LB vserver:

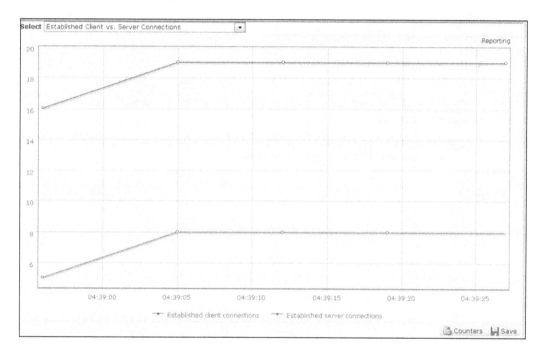

Similarly, CPU and memory utilizations on the device can also be seen on the **Monitoring** and **Reporting** pages. The difference between the **Monitoring** and **Reporting** pages is that the **Monitoring** page provides runtime statistics whereas the **Reporting** page helps collect data for a particular period that can be set to start from the previous hour to the previous year.

The discovery process in the CC is as follows:

1. After adding the maps with the name and other credentials, the CC sends an SNMP Get request for one of the system OIDs:

    □ **For CPU utilization**: 1.3.6.1.4.1.5951.1.1.0.3

    □ **For memory utilization**: 1.3.6.1.4.1.5951.1.1.0.13

2. The CC then establishes an SSH connection to these devices with the username credentials provided while adding a map

3. Once the SSH connection is successful, it will execute a command on the Citrix device to check whether it is a Citrix or a non-Citrix device

4. The CC will then execute a command to configure the community on the discovered device

5. Also, the CC will add its own IP address to the list of trap destinations on the Citrix device; thereby receiving all the traps generated by the device

There's more...

This section will deal with a few tidbits on SNMP and the Citrix CC:

► All the seven PDUs of SNMP, namely `GET`, `GET_NEXT`, `GET_BULK`, `INFORM`, `TRAP`, `RESPONSE`, and `SET`, can be performed to retrieve data from NetScaler

► Whenever the CC is configured, please make sure of the connectivity between NetScaler and the CC

► It is always recommended not to run the CC in tandem with any other SNMP manager, as it might work incorrectly or not work at all

About Packt Publishing

Packt, pronounced 'packed', published its first book "*Mastering phpMyAdmin for Effective MySQL Management*" in April 2004 and subsequently continued to specialize in publishing highly focused books on specific technologies and solutions.

Our books and publications share the experiences of your fellow IT professionals in adapting and customizing today's systems, applications, and frameworks. Our solution based books give you the knowledge and power to customize the software and technologies you're using to get the job done. Packt books are more specific and less general than the IT books you have seen in the past. Our unique business model allows us to bring you more focused information, giving you more of what you need to know, and less of what you don't.

Packt is a modern, yet unique publishing company, which focuses on producing quality, cutting-edge books for communities of developers, administrators, and newbies alike. For more information, please visit our website: www.packtpub.com.

Writing for Packt

We welcome all inquiries from people who are interested in authoring. Book proposals should be sent to author@packtpub.com. If your book idea is still at an early stage and you would like to discuss it first before writing a formal book proposal, contact us; one of our commissioning editors will get in touch with you.

We're not just looking for published authors; if you have strong technical skills but no writing experience, our experienced editors can help you develop a writing career, or simply get some additional reward for your expertise.

Citrix XenServer 6.0 Administration Essential Guide

ISBN: 978-1-849686-16-7   Paperback: 364 pages

Deploy and manage XenServer in your enterprise to create, integrate, manage and automate a virtual datacenter quickly and easily

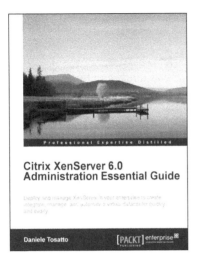

1. This book and eBook will take you through deploying XenServer in your enterprise, and teach you how to create and maintain your datacenter.

2. Manage XenServer and virtual machines using Citrix management tools and the command line.

3. Organize secure access to your infrastructure using role-based access control.

Getting Started with Citrix XenApp 6.5

ISBN: 978-1-849686-66-2   Paperback: 478 pages

Design and implement Citrix farms based on XenApp 6.5

1. Use Citrix management tools to publish applications and resources on client devices with this book and eBook

2. Deploy and optimize XenApp 6.5 on Citrix XenServer, VMware ESX, and Microsoft Hyper-V virtual machines and physical servers

3. Understand new features included in XenApp 6.5 including a brand new chapter on advanced XenApp deployment covering topics such as unattended install of XenApp 6.5, using dynamic data center provisioning, and more

Please check **www.PacktPub.com** for information on our titles

Metasploit Penetration Testing Cookbook

ISBN: 978-1-849517-42-3   Paperback: 268 pages

Over 70 recipes to master the most widely used penetration testing framework

1. More than 80 recipes/practicaltasks that will escalate the reader's knowledge from beginner to an advanced level

2. Special focus on the latest operating systems, exploits, and penetration testing techniques

3. Detailed analysis of third party tools based on the Metasploit framework to enhance the penetration testing experience

BackTrack 5 Wireless Penetration Testing

ISBN: 978-1-849515-58-0   Paperback: 220 pages

Master bleeding edge wireless testing techniques with BackTrack 5.

1. Learn Wireless Penetration Testing with the most recent version of Backtrack

2. The first and only book that covers wireless testing with BackTrack

3. Concepts explained with step-by-step practical sessions and rich illustrations

Please check **www.PacktPub.com** for information on our titles